Poetry Collection

Aminah Rahman

Soul Change

Copyright © Aminah Rahman 2018

All rights reserved. No part of this publication may be reproduced, stored in a retrieval system or transmitted in any form or by any means, electronic, mechanical, audio, visual or otherwise, without prior written permission of the copyright owner. Nor can it be circulated in any form of binding or cover other than that in which it is published and without similar conditions including this condition being imposed on the subsequent purchaser.

ISBN: 978-0-9955093-7-5

Cover Design by Duncan Bamford
http://www.insightillustration.co.uk

Edited by Jan Andersen
http://www.creativecopywriter.org

PERFECT PUBLISHERS LTD
23 Maitland Avenue
Cambridge
CB4 1TA
England
http://www.perfectpublishers.co.uk

Dedication

I would like to dedicate these poems to those who have experienced difficulty in their lives.

Contents

Poem Title	Page
Dedication	iii
Author Bio	vi
Accept Me Please	1
Ain't Gonna Stop	2
Believe	3
Smile for Me	4
I Just Want to Be Happy	5
Your Words	8
What Was It All For?	10
Lost in This World	11
Change	12
Free Syria	13
Go for It	14
Missing You	16
Finding Hope	17
When?	18
I Feel You	19
I AM	20
Twisted Journey	21
Can't Forget	22
Say No to Bullying	23
Cancer Will Not Defeat You	24
Finally Letting Go	25
Refugee	26
I Want Freedom	27
Lost	28
'Oh Grenfell'	29

Author Bio

Aminah is 14 and lives in Cambridge. This is her second collection of poems. Her first book was titled 'Poems by Aminah'.

Aminah was the winner of the Cambridge News and Media Education Awards' Pupil of the Year Award 2017.

Accept Me Please

I may be small, I may be thin,
You only ever judge me by the colour of my skin.
You laugh at my beliefs, you laugh at my scarf,
You always try to ruin my very own path.
You only gimme sorrow, you only gimme hate;
My life's a mess, just look at my state.
Why not help me? Don't criticise another,
Yeah, don't be a hater, try being a lover.
There is nowhere to go, nowhere to turn,
Only go to school 'cos I just wanna learn.
I may be brown; I may be black,
Ruining my books and ruining my rucksack.
I only want a good life, so lend me the keys;
I'm always beggin', yeah, beggin' on my knees.
You only love all discrimination,
Me crying is all a celebration.
I'm brown, you're black, she's mixed, he's white,
Just lemme see diversity – put it in my sight.
You only ever laugh, you only ever tease,
I'm a human too, so accept me please.

Ain't Gonna Stop

Runnin' – runnin' as fast as ever,
Runnin' so fast, it seems like forever,
Dartin' down the streets, tears drip down my face;
No time to wipe them, it's a real big chase.
Eyes wide awake, cannot even blink,
Face is so red, feel like I'm gonna sink.

'Cos I'm runnin' – runnin' as fast as ever,
Runnin' so fast, it seems like forever;
Too scared to stop, I really gotta run,
Complete darkness, can't even find the sun.
Adrenaline's high, but feelin' so low,
Can't I stop runnin'? Nah, it's always a no.

'Cos I'm runnin' – runnin' as fast as ever,
Runnin' so fast, it seems like forever;
Heart is poundin', now too scared to cry,
Yeah, now I see a cliff, but kinda sky-high.
But I jump, yeah, from that scary height;
At least I ain't still in the chaser's sight.

'Cos now I'm swimmin' – swimmin' as slow as ever,
Tryin'a catch my breath, but it seems like forever.

Believe

They don't trust me, they only accuse me;
Trust and forgiveness is the only key.
They think I'm lyin', they don't believe me,
They won't let me speak, they won't let me be free.

I'm tryin'a say the truth, but they don't care,
So much tension just fills the air.
They just blank you, yeah, pretend you're not there.
It's really not nice and it's really not fair.

Doesn't matter what I say, I'm always at fault,
When I try to speak, they only shout "halt!"
It's like they're the sweet and I'm the salt,
Not allowed to speak, trapped in a vault.

Now they don't love, they only hate;
It's unfair cos I hate this state.
Now we ain't good, we used to be mates;
You think nothin' will change, at this rate.

Things will change, I believe,
A good friendship is what I'll achieve,
'Cos don't worry, I got good stuff up my sleeve,
Positivity is what we'll receive.

Smile for Me

You only need to smile for me;
Happiness is the only key
To take you away from the depression,
So, smile for me and let it be a lesson.
A smile is like a disease – it makes its way around;
Sadness is lost, and happiness is found.
Smiling means so much yet costs nothing at all;
Just smile for me – doesn't matter if it's small.
Please, can you smile for me?
And I'm pretty sure that you'll agree
That you feel so happy and feel so bright,
That you'll realise you've found the light.
So, smile through every bit of pain,
'Cos satisfaction is what you'll gain.
Don't let others change your smile;
Don't change it and keep that style,
'Cos smiling doesn't hurt in any single way,
So, smile for me, yeah, smile today.
So, now that you've smiled, spread it around,
'Cos sadness is lost, and happiness is found.

I Just Want to Be Happy

It's not that I don't want to be happy.
Of course, I want to be happy,
But I can't, and it doesn't matter how much I try,
Because faking happiness is just one great lie.

I don't want to have to force a smile on my face
When it's not even real and I'm not even in the right place,
But I have to;
I can't show what is deep inside of me.

People ask me, "Are you okay?"
But I just brush them off with "I'm fine."
'Cos sadness? I don't have time.
I want to be happy, but it's that empty feeling that haunts you,
Scares you – consumes you – and eats away at you.

It's that feeling that never goes away
And it rips your heart in two.
People say you that you should stay positive,
But it's not as simple as that.
It's hard.

I just really want to fill my heart with so much happiness,
It's almost impossible,
But then people always say,
"Impossible spells I'M-POSSIBLE",
But it's not like that, okay?
It was never that easy.

It's that feeling which devours you,
And once it has gone away, it comes back some other time,
'Cos it never let's go of you; it's basically mine.
It leaves me feeling so empty and down
And it feels like I'm missing something somehow.

And I want that 'something' to be happy,
'Cos once I've got that, I'll be free.
I want to be with my friends, but I always have to isolate myself,
'Cos I can't be around people who are so happy when I'm always like this.

I feel so alone, and I can't explain
How heavy I'm feeling and all this pain.
I just need to lift the weights off my shoulders,
Then maybe things will be okay.

Half of the time, it's probably my mind just messing with me.
I just need the happiness' cos that is the key.
Yeah, I'm upset; I don't want to be begging on my knees,
So, just help me please – will you be there for me?

'Cos life isn't easy, not everything is right;
It's this feeling I just want to take out of my sight.
And I roll around in bed, throughout every night,
Thinking about taking a new route, yeah, a new light.

'Cos things will eventually be okay;
It will eventually leave me, and I'll find my way,
'Cos the land of happiness is where I'll stay,
And the land of happiness is where I'll stay.

Your Words

Sometimes, I wish that I could just take
myself away from this world,
'Cos you don't know when to stop,
Or how to respect me,
Or how to speak properly.

I'd love to take myself on a journey
Away from this place,
Where it's just me and myself
And everything else around me freezes.

I just want to go to another place
Where I can break free from this ice
And let it melt in the flames
With which you set me on fire.

'Cos I just need to shut myself from the
outside world
And find the inner peace,
And to get away from you
And your words.

You set me on fire
So now I'll be the ice;
Said I was an idiot, said I was a liar.
I was the sweet cos you were the spice.

So, take me away, somewhere new,
Where your words mean nothing, and none of it's true.
Get rid of this vibe, take me outta the blue,
Take me away to some place new.

What Was It All For?

My special days were the ones with you,
Laughing and smiling all the way.
No secrets kept, everything was true;
Our friendship grew by the day

Those days were short, but now they're long,
Our emotions and feelings broken,
'Cos now it's destroyed and all wrong;
Now our friendship is all a joke.

'Cos you moved on and now you act as if you don't care.
What was it all for – was it all a game?
Love and happiness was what we used to share,
'Cos now it's like a never-ending pain.

And now I watch you walk away from me,
And now you act as if everything is okay.
I asked for an explanation; Did you want to be free?
'Cos you were the one who always made my day.

What was it all for, I ask you?
I asked myself this question so many times,
And now I don't have a clue.

Lost in This World

'Cos I'm lost in this world, don't know where to go;
I wanna explain, but you don't wanna know.
Feelin' kinda heavy, just wanna apologise,
But you won't dare look into my eyes.

I'm lost in this world, don't know where to turn;
Wanna give you my forgiveness, help each other learn.
I know I did wrong and I understand,
But now you're scrapping all the stuff that I had planned.

I'm lost in this world, don't know what to do;
Got some paths to go down – help me choose.
Help me fulfil all my dreams,
Turn my voice into greatness and no more screams

I'm lost in this world; will you help me out?
Hear me out, yeah, hear me out.
Just let the words flow
And then greatness will show.

Change

Wanna go back to the days
When life was alright, go back to our old ways.
Why did things have to change?
Gotta get through the years, but first the days.
We all move on, but it's not the same;
Everything's gone and it's such a shame.
Half of my heart is here, half of it's there;
People just leave you – don't you think it's kinda unfair?
Clocks tick as the seconds go by;
There's stuff to say hello to and sometimes goodbye.
We grow up, aging as the days pass.
I guess not everything's permanent, not everything lasts.
Time runs as quick as ever;
Change won't stop, yeah, it'll go on forever.
It's something we gotta get through,
Discover new things and find what's true,
'Cos change won't leave us; it'll always be there,
Won't ever leave us – it's everywhere.

Free Syria

Free Syria, 'cos hell continues to drop;
It's all just hell – make it stop, make it stop!
Okay, Syria, I know you're falling;
Gonna help you, 'cos I hear you calling.

I feel you and the trickle of your tears,
'Cos the light will shine and soon come near.
It's hard to accept that Syria is doomed,
But always remember, God is with you.

So, Syria, how are you today?
Yeah, it has been seven years; you'll find a way.
None of you deserve to live in fear;
Grey everywhere, make it clear.

Please, Syria, keep your children together.
Just tell them that this won't go on forever.
Please get rid of this evil nightmare,
'Cos only bad vibes fill the air.

Syria, you were the country of light,
But now you've gotta face your darkest nights.
Syria, I'll never forget you; you're always on my mind.
Humanity has fallen, and I hope happiness is what you'll find.

Go for It

Sometimes, it's like we're scared to follow our dreams.
But why is that? What's holding us back?
The people? The emotions? The world?
Some give up before they've even started.
But why? Why do we doubt ourselves?
We are full of magic, full of talent, and it's all going to waste.
There are so many opportunities in life; it's a chase.
Life isn't permanent – you only get one shot at it,
So, just go for it.
We're always holding ourselves back.
You've just got to release yourself, and push all the troubles aside.
This world is full of opportunities – just got to go for it.
Go live something wonderful; don't waste it.
'Cos you only get one shot at life – just go for it.
We focus on our flaws so much that life just walks by.
Explore the world, explore positive vibes.
The nights are young, but the days are old – make the most of the days.
There is so much to see, take yourself away,

'Cos you only get one shot at life; don't waste it.
Find yourself through words, through pictures, through friends,
Through life.
No one will lend it to you; you need to take control.
Explore everything, feed your heart.
Every month is a new chapter,
And you will eventually understand yourself.
Nothing is going to get in our way
As we continue to write our journey.

Missing You

Missing you makes me feel so alone,
Feeling so empty when I see you on my phone,
Drowning in my tears as I wait for you to come back.
When did I last see you? Don't know; I've lost track
Your exit was a mystery;
We hadn't finished our story.
You don't even text me, you don't even call.
Starting to sink as everything falls.
Yeah, I miss you, but you're missing from me.
It's like the horizon yet it's you I can't see.
Always thinking about the years that have passed,
All that shared joy I thought would last.
Always walking down Memory Lane;
Looks like things will never be the same.

Finding Hope

Finding hope has never been easy; it's something that requires determination,
Finding hope in the end is a sensation.
It is difficult, because everything pulls you down.
Hope isn't discovered, but grief is found.
I've spent my time hiding from the world,
But my strength is weakened as my insides are curled.
Finding hope means to clear the clouds.
Finding hope means to discover the town.
Life walks by as I try to search for my escape,
And my tears eventually lose their shape,
Yet many more are released,
'Cos the number of tears is increased.
And I think the time is now to conquer my fears
And let the pain of my past fly away with my tears.
Finding hope may bring you down,
But it can definitely be found.

When?

When will we finally be able to hear the silence?
When will conflict come to its end?
When will people stop walking by struggles?
When will we find happiness?
When will we find peace throughout the world?
When will we speak our thoughts?
When will we open the gates?
When will things stop tearing us apart?
When will **everybody** find happiness?
When will we discover the truth?
When will we understand?
When?

I Feel You

We run through the valleys of truth,
Running past the trees.
I feel your heart beating;
I feel your adrenaline.
We feel the heat from those fires
Of which they dance around.
The moonlight chases us
As we snap the necks of twigs,
Cutting through the wind and falling
forwards.
The wind howls and our footprints leave
their pasts as we run;
Running with empty hearts.
We feel everything, yeah I feel you.
We clasp hands as the clock ticks,
As we run through the valleys of truth.

I AM

I AM me;
Who else would I be?
Why waste my life trying to be someone fake,
When it's such an effort to make?

I AM to stay this way,
Not gonna let myself fade away.
People love for you for who you are;
Being you gets you far

I AM what I see –
No need to look into a mirror; I AM me.
I AM who you see in your eyes.
I AM me; there's no disguise.

I AM.

Twisted Journey

There was so much we shared,
But you've got a twisted journey and then I was scared.
I've got walls that won't come down
And I don't know if your journey is gonna make its way around.
I'm done with all the games you play
And I don't care what you say,
'Cos your twisted journey is gonna get you nowhere.
Don't twist my journey, don't you dare.
Your journey was some nasty treat;
Don't make me go through a repeat.
Now I wish you luck on your twisted journey,
'Cos now I'm on my own journey.

Can't Forget

I can't forget what we used to be.
I see the pain; I wish you could too.
Why have you forgotten me?
It's hard – it's all true.

I can't forget, even after everything that took place.
I'm still missing you.
You wouldn't even show up to my face.
The pain's killing me – you haven't a clue.

The memories don't fade.
You've gone but it's hard to let go,
Then I discovered the game you played.
Thinking about you just makes time slow.

I can't forget what we used to be.
I see the pain; I wish you could too.
Why have you forgotten me?
It's hard – it's all true

Say No to Bullying

You always shout at me, and I start to cry
And you'll never tell me why?
What did I ever do?
Is it 'cos I am smaller than you?
Feeling so low,
Don't know where to go.
Why don't you put yourself in my shoes?
I don't think you realise that your bullying
has given me a permanent bruise.
Mum constantly asks me, "How was your day?"
"I'm fine," I say, but I'm really not okay.
Eventually got a grip, told my friends,
Then the bullying came to an end.
Feeling great, no need to hide,
Because I've got people on my side.
Facing the bullies was a wise choice,
Because now I feel great; I've gained a voice.

Cancer Will Not Defeat You

Cancer may change your life, but don't let it ruin you.
And we are here, for you. TOGETHER.
No, is what we will shout to Cancer.
Courage is what you need. Don't lose this battle.
Enter the world of hope; don't let Cancer defeat you.
Right this minute, we can make a difference.

Let's beat Cancer now.

Finally Letting Go

You're like a star – so close, yet so far away.
I didn't want to lose you now.
Guess I gotta keep my faith, gotta move on.
Was tossing and turning every night;
You were stuck in my head, couldn't get you out.
Everything shattered;
Took me ages to piece things together.
Life was like a puzzle.
You didn't make it easier.
Now I don't want you back,
Not even in a heartbeat,
'Cos
I'm finally letting go.

REFUGEE

Run from the torture that has made its way to Earth.
Escape from your nightmares.
Find your future, find the seas full of change.
Upset is what you are now, but you will find your happiness.
Go – escape from the horror.
Enter the world of love, the world of appreciation.
Emptiness is what fills your heart; join us.

I Want Freedom

I want freedom, to forget about my past,
But the question is, is this gonna last?
I want freedom, to take away the tears and pain,
Don't wanna keep going through this again and again.
I want freedom – is that too much to ask?
Tryin'a be someone new – on my face there's a mask.
I want freedom, to be in some place new;
New doors are what I want to walk through.
I want freedom, for I am me;
A new start is what I want to see.
I want freedom, I will escape,
Just want my future to shape.
I want freedom.

Lost

We get so lost when we pretend we are something different.
We get so lost that sometimes we forget who we are.
We just need to be who we are.
Ourselves.
We are unique in different ways.
You are you.
I am me.
We can put something on this Earth that wasn't here before.
Add this change.
Yes, it takes courage to be yourself.
It's a straight path – follow it.
You don't have to be accepted by others.
You just need to accept yourself.
Because,
We get so lost, when we pretend we are something different.
We get so lost that sometimes we forget who we are.

'Oh Grenfell'

Can't imagine what you went through,
So scary that it doesn't seem true.
Oh Grenfell, you released flames and tears
And now you are our biggest fears.
You printed images of horror that can't be unseen;
Yeah, we saw the horror on our screens.
Oh Grenfell, your flames were so violent;
The screams – so loud that they were so silent.
Absolute chaos as you climbed the tower,
Which you made Britain's darkest hour.
You engulfed the building, tore it apart;
Oh Grenfell, you've broken all hearts.
A year later the screams echo;
Oh Grenfell, horror is all you show.

Milton Keynes UK
Ingram Content Group UK Ltd.
UKHW011821270224
438561UK00005B/557